PROLOGUE

You will say,
"I just like the taste."
But you don't drink for the taste.
You will say,
"I can stop whenever I want."
But you don't stop.
You will say,
"I am fun. I am free. I am alive."
But you are losing yourself.
You will say,
"I don't have a problem."
But you are already here,
reading this book,
asking the question.

Part 1: The Illusion

One won't hurt, two feels right,
Three is warmth, four is light.
Five is wild, six is blurred—
Seven is swearing you're still in control.

Wine is Self-Care and Other Lies

Aromatherapy is self-care.

Wine is procrastinating your breakdown.

I thought I was *"unwinding"*.

Turns out, I was just marinating in bad decisions.

Drinking alone in a candlelight bath isn't relaxation, it's decay with good lighting.

They tell you to drink responsibly

but never define the line—

is it the first glass or the fourth?

or when the room tilts

or when you forget that you were trying to escape?

THE LAST GLASS

A Satirical Poetry Collection on
Sobriety & Self-Deception

Ceri Sian

Satirical Sobriety Press

Copyright © 2025 Ceri Sian

All rights reserved

The characters and events portrayed in this book are fictitious. Any similarity to real persons, living or dead, is coincidental and not intended by the author.

No part of this book may be reproduced, or stored in a retrieval system, or transmitted in any form or by any means, electronic, mechanical, photocopying, recording, or otherwise, without express written permission of the publisher.

First Edition: 2025
Published by: Satirical Sobriety Press

To Alcohol
For making me think I was fun, fearless, and profound when, in reality, I was just loud, reckless, and mispronouncing my own name.

To Sobriety
For showing me that life is still chaotic, awkward, and absurd... but at least now, I remember it.

To my Family
For proving that the best things in life don't come in a bottle (and for putting up with me before I figured that out).

INTRODUCTION

This is not a guide. This is not a self-help book. This is a collection of bad decisions, ghost stories, and hard-won clarity.

It's brutal, biting, and darkly funny—capturing the absurdity of drinking culture, the self-delusions, the shame spirals, and the strange, eerie silence of sobriety. Think if Edgar Allan Poe, Charles Bukowski, and a very pissed-off ex-wine mom wrote a poetry book together.

It starts where most drinking stories do: with fun, freedom, and a little denial. It spirals into regret, lost time, and the kind of mornings that make you Google 'Am I an alcoholic?' at 3 a.m. It doesn't end with a grand redemption arc; rather just an empty glass, a clearer mind, and the unsettling realisation that the hardest part of sobriety isn't quitting. It's staying quit."

Read it front to back, or jump around. Laugh, wince, or share it with someone who needs it. Just know this: if any of this feels too familiar, if you find yourself nodding along or finishing my sentences, then you already know how your story ends.

The only question is how soon you'll stop pretending otherwise.

A Totally Normal Night Out

We were just going for one.
Then one turned into two.
Then two turned into tequila.
Then tequila turned into forgetting
where I put my bag, my phone,
my dignity.

It was fine—
until I woke up,
mouth dry,
stomach in knots,
wondering whose idea it was
to drink an entire bottle
of regret.

(It was mine.)

The Taxi Ride

I swore I wasn't that bad.
I said it over and over, like a spell,
like a prayer.
The driver nudged me awake at my door,
handed me my shoes.
I didn't remember taking them off.

Inside, my phone glowed—

Where are you?
Are you okay?
Jesus Christ, answer me.
I typed back, *I'm fine.*
I typed back, *It was just a long night.*
I typed back—

The message never sent.
I passed out before I hit send.
In the morning,
light too bright,
head too loud,
body too hollow.

The taxi driver had left my shoes neatly by the door.
As if I would need them again.

Making Self-Destruction Look Poetic

Step 1: Order a whisky neat, on the rocks.

Step 2: Hold your glass like a poet with a tragic past.

Step 3: Stare into the distance as if haunted by your own brilliance.

Step 4: Forget you're just a drunk at a bar on a Wednesday.

Step 5: Call it *"living."*

Step 6: Call it *"wild and free."*

Step 7: Call it *"who I am"*.

Step 8: Call your ex.

A Guide to Drinking Socially

Step 1: Set out with good intentions.

Step 2: Have a glass of wine. Feel fine.

Step 3: Order another because *why not?*

Step 4: Lose count. Begin pontificating on life.

Step 5: Say *"I love you guys so much"* to a group of people you met 45 minutes ago.

Step 6: Cry in the toilet about something vague.

Step 7: Wake up with half a kebab in your handbag and one shoe missing.

Step 8: Call that a great night out.

Step 9: Repeat.

One Glass of Wine is Good for You

One glass is good for the heart.

One glass is classy.

One glass pairs well with dinner.

One glass

turns into another,

turns into forgetting dinner,

turns into a mouth that tastes like regret.

But hey,

it's good for the heart,

right?

How to Just Have Just One

Step 1: Order a drink.

Step 2: Sip it slowly.

Step 3: Pause after one.

Step 4: Go home, hydrated and well-rested.

...HAHAHA, NO.

Step 5: Order another because *why not*?

Step 6: Lose track of time, money, and coordination.

Step 7: Wake up questioning your life choices.

Step 8: Vow to be more mindful next time.

Step 9: Repeat for the next decade.

(Unless you're a unicorn. In which case, congrats.)

Convincing Myself I'm Fine

I don't drink that much.
I mean, not every day.
I mean, some days I don't.
I mean, does a few glasses count?
I mean, I could stop if I wanted to.

I mean, could I?

I don't *need* it.
I mean, I just *like* it.
I mean, it's normal, right?
I mean, *everyone drinks.*

I mean, right?

Alcohol Is a Scam, But I Bought It

They said it would make me fun.
They said it would make me wild.
They said it would make me bold, confident, free.
They said it would help me *loosen up,*
help me blend in,
help me belong.
They never said it would make me forget myself.
They never said that, by the end
I wouldn't even miss me.

They Say Wine Gets Better With Age

So why did I always feel worse?

Drinking Like a French Girl

Step 1. Order a glass of wine, effortlessly.
Step 2. Sip slowly, like the heroine in a black and white film.
Step 3. Make eye-contact over the rim. Say something profound.
Step 4. Feel untouchable.
Step 5. Forget that you are not actually French.
Step 6. Order another.
Step 7. Order three more.
Step 8. The night hums, the city leans in, the world turns to velvet.
Step 9. Wake up in a room too bright,
your mouth dry as old paper,
your reflection blurred in a cracked bathroom mirror.
Step 10. French girls wake with lemon water and fresh air.
You wake up looking for paracetamol and silence.
Step 11. The mirror does not lie.
You were never *drinking like a French girl.*
You were just *drinking.*

The Cycle Pours Itself

Drink to celebrate.
Drink to unwind.
Drink because you made it through the week.
Drink because you feel like shit.
Drink to forget drinking.
Drink because stopping feels harder than starting.
Drink.
And then *drink again.*

It doesn't ask.

It doesn't wait.

It just fills the glass before you put it down.

Drink

and then *drink again.*

Part 2: The Spiral

One was fun, two was fine,
Three was slipping past the line.
Four was messy, five was lost—
Six was waking up to count the cost.

It's Not a Problem If…

It's not a problem if you only drink on weekends.
It's not a problem if you drink with friends.
It's not a problem if you drink alone, *but only with netflix on.*
It's not a problem if you drink alone, *but only with music on .*
It's not a problem if you drink alone, *but only to unwind.*
It's not a problem if you drink alone, *but only because you had a bad day.*
It's not a problem if you drink alone, *but only because you had a good day.*
It's not a problem if you drink alone, *but only because it's Tuesday.*
It's not a problem if—
Oh…

I Could Stop If I Wanted To

I could stop if I wanted to.

I just don't want to.

I could stop if I needed to.

I just don't need to.

I could stop, I could stop, I could stop.

I just don't.

Alcohol Maths

1 + 1 = Just two drinks.
2 + 1 = Still reasonable.
3 + 1 = Fine if I drink water after.
4 + 1 = I mean, I've seen people drink way more.
5 + 1 = It's a special occasion.
6 + 1 = It's the weekend.
7 + 1 = I deserve this.
8 + 1 = Tomorrow I'll be better.
9 + 1 = …
No, I don't want to do that math.

The First Time I Lied About How Much I Drank

"How many did you have?"

"Oh, just a couple".

A couple means two.

Three is still close to two.

Four is just a little more than three.

Five is… well.

What's the point of counting now?

"Just a couple."

I said it so easily.

I almost believed it.

What's the Worst That Could Happen?

What's the worst that could happen?
A little headache?
A little regret?
A little, "did I really say that?"
A missed alarm. A missed step.
A message that just says, *dude.*
A taxi receipt to a place I do not live.
Shame, heavy on my shoulders,
buttoned to the throat like a coat I chose.
A stranger, smiling like we have history,
Oh.

This is Why I don't Talk to Sober People

Me: *I don't drink that much.*
Them: *How often?*
Me: *You know, socially.*
Them: *Like...every weekend?*
Me: *Or weekdays. But only after five.*
Them: *Uh-huh.*
Me: *And sometimes at brunch.*
Them: *Right.*
Me: *But never in the morning.*
Them: *Yet.*
Me: *What?*
Them: *Nothing.*
Silence.
The ice in my glass shifts like a tiny earthquake.
The bar hums around us, conversations collapsing into each other.
The air smells like burnt citrus and bad ideas.
I take a sip.
Me: *I don't drink that much.*

The Morning After Routine

The morning comes in sharp edges,
To bright, too loud, too soon.
Regret arrives first, curled in your throat.
Sour as the night before.
Check your phone,
screen glowing like an unblinking eye.

No cracks. No missing pieces.
No messages, only words half remembered.
Typed by another version of you.
Check the group chat—
Blurry photos, laughter spelled in typos.
Did I say that? Did I mean that?

Check your bank balance.
A punishment in numbers.
Swear today is different.
Mean it this time.

Open Deliveroo, order something greasy.
Like an apology.
Netflix hums in the background.
Call it recovery, self care, anything but what it is.
By evening you feel lighter.
Fine.
Outside the streetlights flicker.
The cycle exhales, waiting.

The Rules I Made to Prove I Didn't Have a Problem

1. Only *drink* on weekends.

2. Only *drink* when out with friends.

3. Only *drink* when out with friends,

or if I've had a bad day.

4. Only *drink* when out with friends,

or if I've had a good day.

5. Only *drink* wine, not spirits.

6. Only *drink wine,* not spirits,

unless *it's a special occasion.*

Googling 'Am I an Alcoholic?' at 3 a.m.

I don't drink that much.
I mean, not every day.
I mean, some days I don't.
I mean, does wine even count?
I mean, everyone drinks.

I splash water on my face.
Look in the mirror.
Eyes red. Lips cracked.
A stranger wearing my expression.
I mean, I could stop.
I mean, if I wanted to.
I mean—

Why does my search history already know what I'm about to type?

How Bad Was It, Really?

I mean, it's not like I woke up in jail.
It's not like I lost my job.
It's not like I ruined my life.

It's not like I hurt anyone.

(It's not like I hurt myself.)

It's not like I don't remember.

(It's not like I forgot everything.)

It's not like I forgot everything.

(It's not like I forgot everything.)

Wait.

I'm Just a Fun Drunk

I'm just a fun drunk.
The one who starts the party,
buys the shots,
keeps the energy going.

I'm just a fun drunk.
The one who makes people laugh,
who dances on tables,
who turns any night into a story.

I'm just a fun drunk.
The one who disappears,
who gets lost on the way home,
who wakes up with bruises she can't explain.

I'm just a fun drunk.
Right?

People Who Drink More Than Me (Probably)

I know people who drink *way* more.
The guy from work with whisky in his coffee.
The girl who pre-games before brunch,
who calls it *"a little fizz"* like she's starring in a movie.
The friend who drinks on Mondays.
The friend who drinks alone.
The friend who brings a bottle of wine to the bathroom
because the party is too loud
or too quiet
or too much like the last one.
The friend who—
Oh.
Wait.
That's what they say about me, isn't it?
I laugh,
but no one else does.

I'm Fine

I'm fine,
I'm fine,
I'm fine.

(*I'm lying*).

The words hold.

The words hold.

The words—

Crack.

Part 3: The Last Glass

I don't remember my first drink.
But I remember my last.

Not the sip itself, not the taste,
not the warmth—
but the weight of it.

How heavy it felt in my hand.
How light I thought it would make me.

I stand in front of the mirror,
sober, clear-eyed.
It's still cracked.
But it doesn't distort me anymore.

Side Effects May Include

✓ The headaches, sponsored by bad decisions.

✓ The nausea, *now with extra shame.*

✓ The lost wallets, lost keys, lost dignity, *never to be recovered.*

✓ The texts, *composed by a poet, sent by a fool.*

✓ The bruises, *mysteries in multicolour.*

✓ The 3 a.m. panic, *suddenly fluent in regret.*

✓ The 10 a.m. guilt, *served black, no sugar.*

✓ The hangover that *outlived the high.*

✓ The horror of not knowing what I said,
who I said it to, or why I thought it was profound.

✓ The limited-time-only version of me—
louder, wilder, more tragic,
who swore she was fun,
but mostly just needed saving.

Sobriety is Not a Grand Finale

No fireworks.
No epiphany.
No angelic choir.

Just me.
Just mornings that don't punish.
The nights that don't disappear.

Just a life I no longer have to claw my way back to.

Not perfect.

Not painless.

Not some glorious rebirth.
Just this.

Just me, still here.

Zero Proof

I never counted the first,
but I counted the cost.

Each sip, a fraction of me,
a sum that never balanced.

I thought it stretched to infinity,
but it was always approaching zero.

Now, the proof is in subtraction:
without it, I am whole.

You're So Strong for Quitting

Not really. I just got tired of feeling like shit.

I Didn't Find God, But I Did Find Mornings

I thought sobriety
would split the sky open
bathe me in light
fill my poisoned mind
with something divine.

But all I found
was 6 a.m. stillness,
the hush before the world wakes,
a life no longer slipping,
but settling into my hands.

I didn't find God,
but I found the mornings.
And maybe that's close enough.

I Was Never a Night Owl, I Was Just Drunk

I thought I loved staying out late.
I thought I loved 3 a.m. street food.
I thought I loved afterparties.
I thought I loved sunrise from the wrong side.

Turns out,

I just loved the blur.

The noise.

The distraction.

Turns out,

I was never a night owl.

I was just drunk.

I Didn't Lose My Personality When I Quit Drinking, I Just Finally Met It

I thought quitting would make me less,
that I'd shrink without the swell of a full glass.

But the laughter was never mine—
just noise spilling from an open wound.

Now, I finish books instead of apologies.
I wake up in my own skin,
no longer an echo of last night's mistakes.

Turns out, I wasn't losing anything.
I was just *peeling back the layers*
until I found something real.

What Stays When Alcohol Leaves

The mornings stay.
The memories stay.
The regrets stay,
but they shrink.

The headaches leave.

The nausea leaves.

The shame leaves,

but it takes time.

What stays is *real*.

What stays is *heavy*.

What stays is *you*.

If You See Me Holding a Glass

If you see me holding a glass,
it's coffee.
It's water.
It's overpriced matcha.

It is not regret.

It is not surrender.

It is not the weight of my past

swirling back to the surface.

I gave alcohol

more than enough years of my life.

It doesn't get another one.

I Thought Sobriety Would Be Boring

I thought sobriety would be boring.

Turns out, I just:

✓ Sleep better.

✓ Read books I actually finish.

✓ Show up to things on time.

✓ Remember what I say.

✓ Feel my feelings, even when they suck.

Turns out, I am not boring.

I just no longer confuse

self-destruction

with personality.

This is Enough

No borrowed chaos.
No vanishing hours.
No mornings piecing myself back together.

Just this.
Just the quiet.
Just a life I don't have to translate through regret.

Not dazzling.
Not divine.
Not some great revelation.

Just mine.

And somehow,
for the first time,
That's enough.

The Last Time I Almost Drank

I was fine.
Until I wasn't.
Until the silence stretched too long.
Until the weight of the day felt sharp.
Until I saw someone drinking,
and for a second,
I wanted to be them.
Just one.
Just one.
Just—
I picked up my glass.
It was empty.
A hairline crack down the side.
A fracture so thin, almost invisible.
But I knew how glass breaks,
all at once, then everywhere.
I filled it with water.
I was fine.

Part 4: The Haunting

I quit the drink, but not the ghost,
It lingers here, it haunts the most.
It doesn't pour, it doesn't drown—
It simply waits when no one's around.

I Don't Drink, But It Waits

I don't drink, but it waits.
By the door, by the bed,
in the silence, in my head.
It doesn't knock, it doesn't ask,
it just sits inside the glass.
It knows the nights, the wreckage, the rot,
the things I swore I had forgotten.
It hums like static, low and sweet,
a whisper curling at my feet.

One won't hurt, just one, just one,
same old trick, the same old con.
One is never what it seems,
one is always in-between.

Between today and something worse,
between control and something cursed.
Between the life I swore I'd make,
and everything it wants to take.
So I don't drink, but it waits.
By the door, by the bed,
in the silence, in my head.
It doesn't knock, it doesn't ask,
but still, I tip the empty glass.

Sobriety is a Haunted House

It rattles the ice tray at midnight,
slams the cupboard just to watch you flinch.
The fridge hums a eulogy for lost wine.

Footsteps echo where no one walks—
except maybe your past self,
sloshing through regrets, toasting bad decisions.

The walls whisper in your own voice,
soft as breath, sharp as broken glass.

You reach for something that isn't there—
a glass, a lie, a way back—
but the cupboard is empty,
and the spirits have moved on.

You swear you're alone,
but something still follows,
lingering like gin on an old lover's lips.

It does not knock,
It does not ask.
It simply waits.

Drinking Like a Ghost

I sit at my old barstool.
Watch my past self sip.
Laugh at a joke I don't remember.
Wake up with a headache I don't deserve.

I don't drink,
but the ghost of me does.
She lingers,
lifts the glass to her lips,
whispers *"just one."*

I Used to Drink to Forget

I used to drink to disappear.
To blur the edges.
To loosen the grip of memory.

Now I am staying.
Now I carry every word,
every hour,
every morning, I used to erase.

The streetlight on my skin,
the weight of a stranger's hand on my back,
the sound of a bottle knocking against a sink.

Sobriety gives everything back—
but not all of it feels like a gift.

You're Not Fun Anymore

Them: You're not fun anymore.

Me: *Define fun.*

Them: You used to be wild.

Me: *I used to be reckless.*

Them: You used to drink all night.

Me: *I used to black out.*

Them: You used to be up for anything.

Me: *I used to not know how to say no.*

Them: You used to be one of us.

Me: *I know.*

Cravings Are Just Ghosts

They rise from the floorboards,
from the past,
from nowhere.

They whisper.
They wait.
They call you back.

But they are just ghosts.
They can't touch you
unless you let them.

Alcohol is the Ex That Won't Leave

Ghosts you when you need it,
love-bombs you when you don't.
Says *this time's different*,
but still wears the same bad intentions.
Steals your fun, gaslights your memories,
whispers *I never did that w*hen you swear it did.

Text at midnight just to "*check in*".
Lurks in cafe windows, smug with herbal tea.
Crashes your party.
Won't even pretend to flirt with a gin and tonic.
Orders water with a wink that says, *remember when?*

Promises it won't hurt you again.
Smells like snugness and second changes.
Hangs around long enough
to make you wonder if you were ever really happy,
or just drunk.

It Waits

Part I: The Invitation
It does not knock.
It does not call.
It does not drag me from bed,
claw at my skin,
or rattle the locks.

It only lingers—
low as breath,
thin as dust,
settling in the quiet places
where noone thinks to look.

It waits in the pause before sleep,
in the space between songs,
in the rooms I enter alone.
It waits in my own voice,
whispering my name
like it belongs to it.

It does not knock.
It does not call.
It only waits.
And waits.

Part II: The Resistence

It is patient.
It does not push, does not pull.
It does not need to.

It remembers my weaknesses,
knows the nights that feel too long,
the weight of too much silence.

It waits in the empty glass,
in the phantom taste,
in the hollow space where the habit use to live.

It hums like static, low and sweet,
a whisper curling at my feet.

It is patient.
It does not push,
But I do not reach,
I do not pout.
I do not invite it in.

I turn off the light.
I let the silence stay.
I wait.

The Quiet is Too Loud

It is too quiet.

Too still.

Too sharp.

Too real.

It is too much time.

Too much space.

Too much me.

It is everything alcohol kept away,

and now,

it is here.

Romanticising Drinking

It was never just one
It was never just fun.
It was never just anything,
except inevitable.

The Last Time I Almost Drank

Part I: The Weight of Almost

I was fine
Until I wasn't.
Until the silence stretched too long.
Until I saw someone else drinking,
laughing,
effortless.
For a second,
I wanted to be them.
Just one.
Just one.
Just—

I picked up my glass.
It was empty.
I filled it with water.
I was fine.

Part II: The Quiet

The mornings stay.
The memories stay.
the regrets shrink,
but they stay.

The nausea fades.
The shame loosens its grip,
but not all at once.

What stays is *real.*
What stays is *heavy.*
What stays—
is me.

Yes, I do remember everything now.
No, I don't like all of it.

The Ghost Still Knocks, But I Don't Open the Door

It still whispers.

It still waits.

It still hums through old memories,

taps against the window,

lingers in the corner of my thoughts.

But I do not open the door.

I do not let it in.

I do not let it win.

Alcohol and I Broke Up

And like every toxic ex, it keeps trying to win me back.

The Clouds Are Watching

They drift like cotton candy promises,
sweet and insubstantial,
melting on the tongue of the sky,
leaving nothing but the ache of wanting.

They roll in, soft and innocent,
but watch how they suffocate the sun,
how they swallow the light
with a grin that says, *trust me.*

Step inside, they whisper,
we're weightless we're safe.
But you'll find no footing here,
just the slow, sinking feeling
of falling through yourself.

They say every cloud has a silver lining,
but peel back the pink and tell me,
what do you see underneath?
Because I swear,
it's always grey.

And if you stand still long enough,
you'll hear them murmuring,
just behind your ear-
Come back, Come here,
you were happier here.

It Will Always Wait

It will always wait.
It will always whisper.
It will always be there.
In the silence.
In the empty glass.
In the space between last call and morning.
It will always offer.
It will always promise.
It will always lie.
But I don't have to answer.
I don't have to be.
I let it wait.
Alone.

Part 5: The Escape

No more nights I can't recall,
No more numbers I don't call.
No more shots, no slurred-out fights—
Just longer days and sharper nights

The Glass Stays Empty

I don't pour the drink.
I don't reach for it.
I don't let it reach for me.

Not because I don't hear it *whisper*,
not because it wouldn't be *easy*,
but because I know what comes *after*.
The glass stays empty.
And I *stay*.

Everything I Gained Instead of Alcohol

1. Mornings that don't feel like crime scenes.
2. Memories that don't ghost me by noon.
3. Nights that don't end in whispered apologies to my own reflection.
4. Conversations with receipts—word for word, no cringe.
5. A brain that no longer mutinies.
6. A body that feels less like a rental, more like home.
7. A life I don't need to drink to tolerate.

The Drink I Don't Pour

It would be easy.
A glass.
A sip.
A slow unravelling.
It would be easy.
To lean back into the blur,
to loosen the sharp edges,
to let go of the weight
of remembering.

But I do not pour the drink.

And because of that,
I get to stay.

I Thought I'd Miss Drinking

I thought I'd miss the taste.

The burn, the bite, the familiar poison.

I don't.

I thought I'd miss the fun.

The loud laughter, the reckless dancing.

I don't.

I thought I'd miss the chaos.

The nights that blurred into mornings,

the stories I couldn't remember,

I do.

But only a little.

Now, I find solace in the quiet dawns,

in the clarity of unclouded thoughts,

in a life that's mine to hold

steady and true.

I thought I'd miss drinking more than I do.

Turns out, I don't miss losing myself.

I only miss the noise,

silence I've learned

is its own kind of music.

People Who Are Offended By My Sobriety Are Suspicious

If you don't care what I drink,
you don't care what I drink.

If you do care what I drink,
why do you care?

I Am No Longer At War

For years,
I lived in a body
that fought itself.
Pushed against itself.
Wanted more,
wanted less,
wanted out.

Now,
there is no war.
Just space.
Just breath.
Just me.

Noone Talks About the Loneliness?

Everyone talks about clarity.
Peace.
Self-respect.
Healing.

No one talks about the silence.
The space left behind.
The way the world still drinks without you.
No one talks about the nights
where you realise
it wasn't the alcohol you miss—
it's the version of you
that didn't have to feel this much.

It Turns Out, I Wasn't Actually That Fun

I was the wild one,
the shot-taker, the night-stretcher,
the one who turned last call into an arguement,
and hangovers into a personality trait.

Turns out, *I was just loud.*
Just a girl with a bottle for a microphone,
on a stage built from bad decisions,
and an audience too drunk to notice
the punchlines were all confessions.

It wasn't fun.
It was just motion,
spinning fast enough to keep the emptiness dizzy.
Turns out, *I wasn't the life of the party,*
just the ghost who refused to leave.

How People React When You Say You Don't Drink

1. The Over-Apologiser: *"I'm so sorry, I didn't know."*

2. The Investigator: *"But like...why?"*

3. The Self-Justifier: *"I mean, I don't drink that much either."*

4. The Peer Pressure Enthusiast: *"You can just have one though, right?"*

5. The Quiet one: *They don't say anything, but you can tell they're thinking about their own drinking now.*

The Real Reason I Stopped Drinking

Because I was way too good at it.

The Price of Remembering

I used to drink to disappear.
To slip through the cracks
between yesterday and never.

Now I stay.

Now I know.

Now I gather every word,

every hour,

every morning I once let shatter.

Sobriety gives everything back—

but some of it is returned in pieces.

Some of it is still sharp.

Some of it still cuts when I hold it too tight.

But even *broken glass* catches the light.

ACKNOWLEDGEMENTS

To my friends who never pressured me to *"just have one,"* you are rare, and I love you for it. To everyone who sent a *"Wanna go for drinks?"* text and got *"Let's get coffee instead"*, thank you for meeting me where I am.

To the sober and sober-curious community. Whether you're years in, just starting, or still Googling *"Am I an alcoholic?"* at 3 a.m, this book is for you. Finally, to alcohol. For the bad decisions, questionable memories, and enough material for an entire book.

If you need help with drinking, you are not alone. There is support available, and it is never to late to reach out:

Alcoholics Anonymous (AA): www.aa.org
SMART Recovery: www.smartrecovery.org
NHS Alcohol support (UK): www.nhs.uk/live-well/alcohol-advice/

ABOUT THE AUTHOR

Ceri Sian

Ceri Sian is a writer, satirist, and recovering expert in bad decisions. Once convinced that wine was self-care and tequila was a personality trait, she now spends her time proving that life is still chaotic, hilarious, and deeply absurd, even without alcohol.

When not writing, she's raising her children, pursuing her Doctorate in Chester and drinking enough coffee to power a small city. She believes sobriety is the ultimate plot twist, mornings are still overrated and the best things in life don't come in a bottle.

This is her first poetry collection, but probably not her last.

Printed in Great Britain
by Amazon